D0945432

DK READERS

Level 1

Level 2

A Note to Parents

DK READERS is a compelling program for beginning readers, designed in conjunction with leading literacy experts, including Dr. Linda Gambrell, Distinguished Professor of Education at Clemson University. Dr. Gambrell has served as President of the National Reading Conference, the College Reading Association, and the International Reading Association.

Beautiful illustrations and superb full-color photographs combine with engaging, easy-to-read stories to offer a fresh approach to each subject in the series. Each DK READER is guaranteed to capture a child's interest while developing his or her reading skills, general knowledge, and love of reading.

The five levels of DK READERS are aimed at different reading abilities, enabling you to choose the books that are exactly right for your child:

Pre-level 1: Learning to read
Level 1: Beginning to read
Level 2: Beginning to read alone
Level 3: Reading alone
Level 4: Proficient readers

The "normal" age at which a child begins to read can be anywhere from three to eight years old. Adult participation through the lower levels is very helpful for providing encouragement, discussing storylines, and sounding out unfamiliar words.

No matter which level you select, you can be sure that you are helping your child learn to read, then read to learn!

LONDON, NEW YORK, MUNICH,
MELBOURNE, AND DELHI

Project Editors Naia Bray-Moffatt,
Deborah Murrell
Art Editor Jane Horne
U.S. Editor Regina Kahney
Production editor Siu Chan
Jacket Designer Natalie Godwin
Illustrator Peter Dennis
Publishing Manager Bridget Giles

Reading Consultant
Linda B. Gambrell, Ph.D
Research Source
Jamestown–Yorktown Foundation, Virginia

First American edition, 2000
This edition, 2009
10 11 12 13 10 9 8 7 6 5 4 3 2
Published in the United States by DK Publishing
375 Hudson Street, New York, New York 10014

Copyright © 2000 Dorling Kindersley Limited

All rights reserved under International and Pan-American Copyright
Conventions. No part of this publication may be reproduced, stored
in a retrieval system, or transmitted in any form or by any means,
electronic, mechanical, photocopying, recording, or otherwise,
without the prior written permission of the copyright owner.

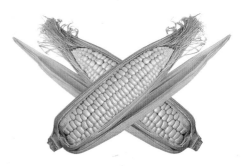

Published in Great Britain by Dorling Kindersley Limited

DK books are available at special discounts when purchased
in bulk for sales promotions, premiums,
fund-raising, or educational use.
For details, contact: DK Publishing Special Markets
375 Hudson Street, New York, New York 10014
SpecialSales@dk.com

A catalog record for this book is available
from the Library of Congress

ISBN: 978-0-7566-5611-9 (pb)
ISBN: 978-0-7566-5612-6 (plc)

Color reproduction by Colourscan, Singapore
Printed and bound in China by L. Rex Printing Co. Ltd.

The publisher would like to thank the following for
their kind permission to reproduce their photographs:
Key: c=center; t=top; b=bottom; l=left; r=right
Bridgeman Art Library: Private Collection 2 t, 32 tl;
Science Museum, London 32 cl; **J. Allan Cash Ltd.:** 31; **Corbis:**
Bettmann 3, 32 cr, Harholdt 10, Richard T. Nowitz 33, Tim Wright
25 b; **Fine Art Photographic Library Ltd.:** Private Collection 28;
Jamestown-Yorktown Foundation: 7 b, 32 bl; **Borough Council of
King's Lynn and West Norfolk:** 2 b, 32 br; **Paul Weston:** 5 b.
Front jacket: Library of Congress: Prints & Photographs Division.
All other images © Dorling Kindersley
For further information see: www.dkimages.com

Discover more at
www.dk.com

DK **READERS**

BEGINNING TO READ ALONE
2

The Story of Pocahontas

Written by Caryn Jenner

DK Publishing

"I saw pale strangers!"
A hunter returned
to the Indian village
shouting the news.
"They are building a town."

Pocahontas ran to listen.
"Isn't it exciting, Father?"
said Pocahontas.
Her father, Chief Powhatan,
frowned. "We shall see."

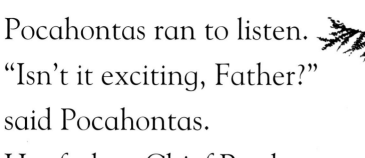

A long journey

The first settlers took five months to sail from England to America. They arrived in April 1607.

Powhatan sent Pocahontas
and a group of scouts
to the strangers' town.
They walked silently,
hiding among the trees.
Everything about the settlers
was strange.
Some even had hair on their faces!

Bravely, Pocahontas stepped forward
and greeted them with a smile.
A hairy-faced man smiled back.

The new land
The settlers unloaded
their ships and set out
to explore America.
They hoped to find
gold and other riches.

Pocahontas made many visits
to the settlers' town.
She learned that the smiling man
with the hairy face was
Captain John Smith.
The settlers were from England.
They called their new home
Jamestown, after their ruler,
King James.

Sometimes Pocahontas brought
food for the hungry settlers.
They knew many things,
but they did not know
how to grow corn.

Pocahontas liked the settlers,
but many Indians did not.
Chief Powhatan held a meeting.
"The pale strangers mean trouble,"
he told his people.
"If we attack them, they will go away."
"Father, let's be friends with them,"
said Pocahontas.
"Strangers take our land,"
said Powhatan.
"They cannot be trusted."

Chief Powhatan
Pocahontas's father, Powhatan, was chief of more than 14,000 Indians. His tribes lived in many nearby villages.

11

Powhatan's warriors took
Captain Smith as a prisoner.

"Let him go, Father,"
Pocahontas pleaded.
"No," said Powhatan.
"We must show the strangers
that there are a great many of us.
Then they will not fight us."

The warriors took Smith
to see many Indian villages.
The Indians treated him as a guest.
But they would not let him go free.

One day, Powhatan held a feast
in his own village.
Pocahontas watched as the warriors
arrived with Captain Smith.
Powhatan gave a signal.
Suddenly, the warriors
swung their clubs over Smith's head.

Pocahontas raced forward.

"Stop!" she shouted.

"Don't kill him!"

Powhatan ordered the warriors
to put down their clubs.

"You are lucky," he told Smith.

"My daughter has saved your life."

Pocahontas and John Smith
became friends.
Smith taught Pocahontas
to speak English.
She taught him some Indian words.
Pocahontas asked her father
to help the settlers.
They were not used
to the harsh winter.

Chief Powhatan gave them food
from the autumn harvest.
The settlers were grateful.
For a while,
the Indians and settlers
lived in peace.

One day, another ship arrived,
bringing more English settlers.
The new settlers took more land.
This made Powhatan angry.
Pocahontas and Captain Smith
tried to keep the peace.
But the Indians and the settlers
did not like each other.

Winter came again.
Captain Smith wanted to trade
English goods for food.
He camped near
Powhatan's village.

Pocahontas heard her father
plan to attack the camp.

Trading for food

The hungry settlers had goods from England for trading. They wanted the Indians to give them corn and other food in return.

Pocahontas waited
until everyone was asleep.
Then she walked
through the wind and snow
to warn her friend.
"You have saved me again,
Pocahontas," said Smith.

Many seasons passed.
Pocahontas grew into
a young woman
and moved to a new village.
She heard that her friend,
John Smith, had died.
The Indians and settlers
continued to fight.

One day, an English ship
docked near the village.
Pocahontas went on board to visit.
The ship's captain, Captain Argall,
would not let her leave.
She was kidnapped!

Captain Argall took Pocahontas
to a new town near Jamestown.
Pocahontas learned to act
like a settler.
She wore heavy cloth dresses
and a cap on her head.

She went to church
with her new friends.
They baptized her and gave her
the English name Rebecca.

The settlers' church

Church was very
important to the settlers,
and Pocahontas was
baptized into the
Christian religion.

All of the settlers liked Pocahontas,
especially a man named John Rolfe.
Pocahontas wanted to marry him.
Powhatan made peace
with the settlers to celebrate
his daughter's marriage.
It was the best wedding present
Pocahontas could have.
Pocahontas and her husband
had a baby named Thomas.
They all sailed
across the ocean
to visit England.

"What do you think of England?"
John Rolfe asked his wife.
"There are so many people!"
Pocahontas replied.
The people stared at Pocahontas.
They had never seen
an Indian before.
She remembered
how she had stared
when she first saw the settlers.
So she just smiled.

A visit to England
In England, many people
wanted to meet
Pocahontas and
learn about America.

King James and Queen Anne
thought Pocahontas was charming.

Pocahontas had been in England
for several months
when she became ill.
One day, she had a surprise visitor.

It was Captain Smith!

"You're alive!" gasped Pocahontas.

"Alive and well," Smith replied.

"You must get well, too."

Sadly, Pocahontas did not get better.

She was only 21 years old
when she died.

Pocahontas helped to bring
peace and friendship between
the settlers and Indians in America.

A memorial

This statue stands in
Gravesend, England,
where Pocahontas is buried.
She is remembered as a
brave and clever girl.

Indians and Settlers

In 1492, Christopher Columbus set sail for India. He landed on America instead! But he called the Native Americans "Indians."

Pocahontas was about eleven years old when the settlers arrived in Jamestown in 1607. Pocahontas is a nickname that means "playful." Her real name was Matoaka.

When the Puritans of England heard about Jamestown, they decided to sail to America, too. Their ship, the *Mayflower*, landed in Plymouth, Massachusetts, in 1620.

Pocahontas's son, Thomas, grew up in England. As an adult, he returned to live in America on land given to him by his grandfather, Chief Powhatan.

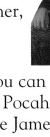

You can visit a re-creation of Pocahontas's village and the Jamestown settlement near the original site in Virginia.

Index

WITHDRAWN

**Indianapolis
Marion County
Public Library**

**Renew by Phone
269-5222**

**Renew on the Web
www.imcpl.org**

For General Library Information
please call 269-1700

DEMCO